A Good Day to Die

Haiku in Traditional Form

CARL WEAVER

Copyright 2015 by Carl Weaver. All rights reserved.
Published by Broken Column Press.
BrokenColumnPress.com
ISBN: 978-0-9966341-0-6

Introduction

Most people know what haiku is – a traditional form of Japanese poetry composed in three lines of specified lengths of five, seven, and five syllables. Indeed, it is a style that seems simplistic and short and is often not given sufficient study by students of modern verse.

Some modern poets disregard this strict structure and simply write short lines of about those lengths, not worrying too much about the formal structure. I would argue that the form defines the poetry, and that the reflections contained within the bounds of the inked page are partly defined by the structure, rather than freed by its absence.

For my own purposes, I decided to stick as close to the original structure as possible. However, I did make some innovations in deviating from traditional topics. Haiku originated in Tokugawa-era Japan and was considered a contemplative art. Many of the subjects stemmed from observations the author made about the world around him, including nature, seasons, animal life, other people, and even his own changing emotional state. To this I added some poems of passion and romance, which is not technically outside the scope of haiku but is definitely not among the traditional topics, as they are also meditations on a moment separated from the rest of existence.

The haiku form is restricting and many writers find it difficult to use, compared to the open format of free verse poetry. The task with almost any poem is to use words economically and to paint a picture that is more than the sum of its parts. Haiku is no exception. In a mere 17 syllables, the writer has to express an idea, moment or emotion without using concrete, direct language. As such, there are likely no individual haiku that speak to an entire cross-section of society the way Allen Ginsberg's *Howl* or Walt Whitman's *I Sing the Body Electric* might.

As such, haiku is rather limited, more appropriate for a single idea or contemplation. The subjects of haiku are most often expressed in reference to nature or man's interaction with nature: season, weather, landscape, fauna and flora. Two images or ideas are brought together in the lines and related through language and description. The haiku master Matsuo Bashō has many excellent examples of this technique:

> Wrapping dumplings in
> Bamboo leaves, with one finger
> She tidies the hair

> The whole family
> All with white hair and canes
> Visiting graves

> On Buddha's birthday
> A spotted fawn is born –
> Just like that

A haiku is a moment expressed, a singularity of experience, somewhat contradictory, and yet wholly relatable on some level. Like other forms of poetry, it speaks to the human experience, not to a sense of perfection or an ideal of some sort. It brings together the richness and sorrow of our lives, combining the sad and happy, the pleasure and fear, into a small part of one unified gestalt that encompasses all experience.

The haiku in this book is there to enjoy and hopefully find some meaning in. Sir Philip Sidney wrote that the purpose of poetry was to delight and entertain. That is about the highest goal a writer can have.

The history of haiku in American culture goes back to the 1950s, when poets such as Gary Snyder and Allen Ginsberg made the style more recognizable. However, the real history of the form stretches back much farther.

As far back as the 7th century, Japanese poetry included a style whose line lengths were dictated by varying number of syllables. An early style, and one of the more familiar styles, *waka*, consisted of lines of 5-7-5-7-7 syllables. This style was eventually more formalized and today is known as *tanka*. Later, this style was adapted to be a co-production of two or more poets, often one writing the first three lines and another writing the final couplet. These collaborative projects, known as *renga*, could be quite long, as more poets got involved, and around the 15th or 16th century, devolved into being a series of word plays and games of clever wordsmithing, rather than what we would necessarily think of as a fine art.

The poetry master Matsunaga Teitoku revived the *tanka* and *renga* in the 17th century and made them, once again, more sophisticated art forms. His student, Mastuo Basho, the now-famous poet, adapted the *tanka* style further, cutting off the last two lines, and giving us what we have today – the 5-7-5 syllable structure, something he termed as *haikai*. It was not until the mid-19th century that Masaok Shiki formalized the style further and renamed it haiku.

The title of this book comes from the adoption of haiku as one of the contemplative arts used by samurai to focus their energies before venturing into combat. In their attempt to embrace the certainty of death and enter into it consciously, some would meditate on how that day was a good day to die and write death poems to mark the occasion.

Writers and readers alike have delighted in both the simplicity and the complexity of haiku, the seemingly opposite aspects like two hands grasping the same sword, neither able to wield it without the other.

Carl Weaver
June 2015
Arlington, Virginia

1.

Midday summer sun
Lazy turtles bask in warmth
Lunchtime flirtation

2.

Morning storm showers
Hard rain plinking on glass panes
Springtime symphony

3.

Singsong cicadas
Warm evening before autumn
Evening serenade

4.

Summer's last vestige
Cool mist in western mountains
Streaming shafts of light

5.

The cool rain has washed
Cherry blossoms from the trees
Slow pink river flows

6.

Old friends rekindle
Long-spent embers of lost love
Romance remembered

7.

A passionate kiss
Springtime blossom canopy
End or beginning?

8.

Long autumn shadows
Hands touch, a romance blossoms
Lost in sweet kisses

9.

Love has flown away
Like autumn geese on fleet wing
Rain clouds fill my heart

10.

I smell long ago
Your hair, sweat, love, supple neck,
Eyes closed, rosebud lips

11.

Winter's precipice
Cool nights and dark afternoons
My breath, a fog

12.

All my yesterdays,
Stolen by time, float by like
Milkweed in the breeze

13.

Rain changing to snow
Dark morning awash in chill
Winter's renewal

14.

Tiny buds lost to
Nature's ice-clad recesses
Winter's calling card

15.

Sunlight on fresh snow
Early morning revelry
A jaybird calls out

16.

Black on clouded sky
Migrating birds flit southward
A gentle snow falls

17.

Warm spell coaxes buds
Cold creeps in with thief's prowess
Winter's greedy take

18.

A winter romance
Words flow from lips, eyes flirting
Warm hearts in cold air

19.

A fleeting moment
Lips embrace, resist the chilled air
Winter romance sparked

20.

Fallen leaves in stream
A flotilla of flora
On rippled sunlight

21.

Dawn contemplation
A shaft of sunlight through clouds
Wonder, beauty, awe

22.

A finality
Events not yet transpired
A bud plucked, ungrown

23.

Nose cold from raindrops
A harbinger approaches
Winter's kiss afoot

24.

Meeting new choices
Fearless, a samurai's life
A good day to die

25.

Showers from the west
The sun absent three days now
Cool fingers, warm heart

26.

All the birds have gone
Silent tide pool edged with ice
Water laps, breeze blows

27.

A new morning breaks
Opportunity abounds
The sun behind clouds

28.

Sad letter arrives
A friend's wishes unfulfilled
My heart, a rice bowl

29.

A release, a gasp
Blind, under covers, hands grope
Lips meet, love renewed

30.

Cold, slow morning rain
Dampness permeates and chills
Friendship's warmth renews

31.

Overcast morning
A cold wind blows, rustles hair
Brown leaves fall from limbs

32.

Lost loves plague my heart
Buddhist teachings reinforced
Grief impermanent

33.

Fingers interlaced
Whispered romance through red hair
Your neck all kisses

34.

A low winter sun
Drives off permeating chill
The frost sublimates

35.

Afternoon's golden rays
The low sun with long shadows
My lips, nose frozen

36.

Like birds of springtime
My heart has returned on wing
Warm in the cool air

37.

Breath like morning fog
A cloud of birds takes flight
My spirit returned

38.

A romance blossoms
Budding peonies glimmer
In warm springtime rain

39.

Promise of morning
Opportunity abounds
My path untrodden

40.

Lost in an embrace
A mockingbird calls its songs
Your lips rich like wine

41.

Your lips, a refuge
My tomorrows forgotten
Afternoon sweetness

42.

Wordless dialog
An embrace of lips, clasped hands
Birdsong in my heart

43.

The heat oppressive
Song of cicadas rises
The day a mirage

44.

A landscape transformed
The path I walk has aged, changed
Since last I was here

45.

Dessert smiles, sweetness
All life's moments behind me
Evening flirtation

46.

Finding the Buddha
Drip-drap water tap trickle
A smile, perfect calm

47.

Your voice, a whisper
A songbird's call carried on
The cool morning breeze

48.

Captivating eyes
Soft blue and crystal clear like
Norwegian water

49.

New sense of sweetness
Shared laughter, a joke retold
Smiling in my heart

50.

Morning majesty
God's daily gift of more light
The sun behind clouds

51.

Calm overcast dawn
Clouds like silk over sun's rays
Winter's approach

52.

Temple of the heart
Light through clouds - sunlit columns
The heart grows stronger

53.

Soft rays at sunset
Pink and orange fingers splay
A moment's treasure

54.

Summer lunch chatter
Hum of cicadas heightens
Respite from heat wave

55.

Eight flames fight darkness
A miracle, light renewed
Conquest remembered

56.

Your kisses smolder
A spike of passion excites
My desire heightened

57.

A fog descending,
Cool mist from light gray heavens
Penetrating chill

58.

Summer remembered
Warmth gone, like so many birds
Now chill and shivers

59.

Our fingers enmeshed,
Feeling each other's warm heart
Kissing in cold night

60.

Soft snow flakes float down
Winter's return a beacon
Three cold months await

61.

Forgotten lost loves,
To each I raise my sake
Glad the past is gone

62.

You have flown, gone now
Only memories remain
Your scent in my sheets

63.

Morning renewal
A daily trove of blessings
My heart a fountain

64.

Thick fog descended
The mist leaves its calling cards
One million dew drops

65.

A dance of passion
Bodies entwined, connected
Like grapevine tendrils

66.

Moss thick around trees
Every direction due north
A confused laughter

67.

The sunlight of dawn
Fingers of darkness from trees
Frost steams from grass

68.

Her hair red, lips red,
Skin pale in the evening light
My heart flower blooms

69.

A soft breeze starts up
Brown leaves fall gently to ground
Cool moisture in air

70.

Lips tingle when kissed
Neck a waiting oasis
I drink you fully

71.

Approaching nighttime
Tears and sorrow fill the room
Adieu, my old friend

72.

Waking in evening
I still taste you on my lips,
Still see your clear eyes

73.

Late blooming winter
Buds on trees appear, but doomed
By the coming frost

74.

The traffic aroused,
Woken from slumber, splashing
Morning gutter rain

75.

Sweet morning kisses
Awakened by your soft touch
Your skin warm on mine

76.

Moments of glory
My nighttime spent in embrace
Lost in your love's scent

77.

A morning sprinkle
Water beads on waxen leaves
My nose cold, heart warm

78.

Cool rain brings blue thoughts
Plinking against my window
Remembered loss, grief

79.

Last time I saw you
We were no longer in love
I could not find words

80.

That time before love
When all seems golden, perfect
Before things get tough

81.

This place I visit
A place I knew in my youth
No longer my home

82.

Kisses on your neck
Under a mantle of leaves
Your hands in my coat

83.

Sparrows in cold rain
Sit still on staggered fenceposts,
Until not, then gone!

84.

Old friends uniting
Warm hugs, eager discussion
Like no time has passed

85.

A nip of sake
The day's cold mantle shrugged off
Regained bravado

86.
Rainfall rhapsody
Plinking, tapping on windscreen
Wipers chime in - swish!

87.
Lying together
Feeling your gaze upon me
Breaths in unison

88.
My hands black with soot
My love grew in a box car
Your blonde hair streaming

89.
Late night flirtation
A quiet walk, our hands touch
Your lips inviting

90.
Steam rising from tea
Afternoon contemplation
Emptiness returned

91.

Your lips electric
Touching your waist, hands pressing
Lost in your kisses

92.

Black hair shining like
Moonlight in your eyes, longing
My hand on your waist

93.

White frost in morning
Crystal-capped nature display
My breath a warm fog

94.

The smell of breakfast,
The warm kitchen a refuge
Against cold mornings

95.

Silken evening clouds
Lit by gradation against
Winter's dusken sky

96.
My heart could be smashed
By a woman as you are
I could fall in love

97.
Breakfast oatmeal
Delicious mealtime flirting
Blue eyes, crystal heart

98.
If my heart opens
You could swallow the whole thing
In one single breath

99.
A fortress we built
Against the dark foes of love
Your neck, my solace

100.
Sliver of red sky
Cut across morning darkness
A knife slit through clouds

101.

A winter rosebud
Lips pursed, ready to meet mine
My face cold, then warm

102.

Morning snow blanket
All quiet, gentle, downy
A sparrow flits by

103.

Afternoon sunshine
Diffused by thin cloud cover
Slow snow melt trickle

104.

After our passion
I stroke your hair, smiles, kisses
Our breaths as one

105.

Heavy snow falling
Pine boughs weighed down, tipping down,
Reverent bowing

106.
Snowy footprints left
Birds on the walkway, now gone
Snow falls and hides tracks

107.
Your neck, so tender
Each kiss an ode to longing
Sweet like summer rain

108.
Laughter among friends
Wine glasses poured to the brim
Purple-stained lips smile

109.
Lost book of haiku
My search ends with empty hands
Outside - moon and stars

110.
Hesitant snowstorm
White morning blanket outside
Muffled bird singsong

111.

Your smile a bouquet
My life in bloom around you
My heart a lotus

112.

Morning sun obscured
Bright spot through blanket of clouds
Birds fly off bare tree

113.

Hot night in August
Thousand-frog chorus sounds off
Moon glows behind clouds

114.

The morning fog low
Quiet dawn with obscured sun
Hidden mountain home

115.

Auburn glow in east
Morning moon low in the sky
Missing your soft touch

116.
Your lips are what I
Wake from my dreams to think of,
Lost, like a sunrise

About Carl Weaver

Carl Weaver is a writer and editor based in the Washington, DC area. He became interested in poetry at an early age and in haiku in college, when he was introduced to the study of Zen and Samurai culture. He is the author of *Next Life in the Afternoon: A Journey through Thailand*, a memoir of traveling through Thailand and staying in Buddhist monasteries in an effort to become a monk.